Part O

God, the Father: The Creator, who watches over His creation

*Splendour and majesty
are before Him
strength and glory are in
His sanctuary.
…ascribe to the Lord
glory and strength.
Ascribe to the Lord the
Glory due to his name
…worship the Lord in
the splendour of His holiness.*

Ps. 96 : 6-9

Father

Heavenly Father,
You are the God who watches day and night,
who never sleeps but cares for all you have created.
You ask me to be your child, to look to you for everything.
I know you have the power in which you organise the universe,
the power in which you involve me to play my part,
to play that part responsibly.
It is imperative that I trust you in all things,
that I recognise you as my Maker, creator and Father, as being of love
But in the essence of love lies the power that conquers
not by force but by sacrifice
By calling me to be your child you make me co-heir
in serving my brothers and sisters with sacrifice.
I know love is many things but that sacrificial love is nearest in
my quest to imitate the love of Jesus
By His word and example I have the life-pattern by which you
want me to live.
And though his own did not understand Him
I have now the Holy Spirit to illuminate my mind and heart
to lead me into all truth
Help me, Heavenly Father, to look to you in all things,
to trust in love,
to live by faith, to be your child.
Amen.

(ET)

Beyond

The evidence
of Your Fatherly presence
is everywhere
Your breath
is upon my life.
You hover over me
You lay Your hand
upon me.
You hold me
in Your arms
You warm my heart
You are deep within me
the very ground
of my being
You are more real
than reality
You are beyond
all words
beyond all images
and definitions
You are beyond,
yet very present
here and now
in Christ.

(DW)

Walking With God

Prayers and meditations for today
SR. ELIZABETH TUTTLE PBVM
&
DENNIS WRIGLEY
of the
Maranatha Community

Published and distributed by RoperPenberthy Publishing Limited,
P.O. Box 545, Horsham RH12 4QW www.roperpenberthy.co.uk
All enquiries to the publishers.

ISBN   978-1-903905-33-3

All scriptures quoted are from the Holy Bible, New International Version,
copyright, 1973, 1978, 1984 by the
INTERNATIONAL BIBLE SOCIETY
Used by permission of Hodder and Stoughton Ltd
OR from the New Jerusalem Bible copyright Darton Longman and Todd

Walking with God

Contents

Walking with God

Foreword

"For its inspiration this remarkable book of prayers draws on two Christian traditions - and it is all the more powerful for that reason. Alfred Lord Tennyson famously wrote that "more things are wrought by prayer than this world ever dreams" but we frequently dismiss the powerful efficacy of prayer, simply preferring to rely on our own strength instead.

Sister Elizabeth and Dennis Wrigley are two people who have experienced the full power of prayer and this lovely collection of their meditations and prayers reflects the intimacy of their relationship with God. 'Walking with God' will be an immense inspiration to many." **Professor the Lord Alton of Liverpool**

Preface

"As the title suggests, this book will take you on a journey. The prayers, reflections and meditations will draw you more deeply into the beautiful mystery of the Trinitarian God. By allowing the words to become your own, you will indeed walk with God and also come to realise more fully that God is present in every aspect and moment of life. Pondering what is written here will enable you to appreciate afresh the Fatherhood of God the Creator, the majesty of God the Son – 'the name beyond all others' – and the vibrancy of God the Holy Spirit. Sr. Elizabeth Tuttle and Dennis Wrigley have demonstrated well that Christians of different traditions can achieve wonderful things by working together to put prayer and the things of God in first place." **Rt. Rev. Arthur Roche, Bishop of Leeds**

This book is jointly written by Dennis Wrigley, the Leader and Co-Founder of the Maranatha Community and Sister Elizabeth Tuttle PBVM, a Presentation Sister who has also played a leading role in Maranatha for many years. It is a fusion of the inspiration given to a Catholic Sister and a Protestant layman.

Walking With God

*Who may ascend the hill
of the Lord?
Who may stand in his holy place?
He who has clean hands
and a pure heart…
He will receive blessings
from the Lord*

Ps. 24 : 3-4a; 5a

Simplicity

Let me know in my heart, Lord
that it doesn't matter
if I live or die,
because I am yours
that it doesn't matter
where I am
as long as I am with you.

This will be my contentment,
my peace,
my life fulfilled.

The only thing that really matters, Father
is my love for you,
because this love
springs from your love,
just as the morning
springs out of the night
and spring follows winter –
the everlasting cycle of your law.
Enable my love to grow and flow
and spread its healing into the world.

Let it be the fruit of the treasures
come from you.

(ET)

Travelling

I keep on travelling
and the pace is fast
the journey is long
how long will it last?
I stumble and fall
but You raise me up
I am filled with exhaustion
but You give me new strength
I question direction
You bid me to trust
You stride out before me
in confident haste,
Your movement invested
with urgent intent
as I run and I scramble
over roughest terrain
and claw up the cliffs
on precipitous paths.
There is scarce time
to question
the route You are taking
or to fully take in
the wonders and signs
the forms and the images
that flash through my mind.
The rapid encounters
the rush and the heartbeat,
a way that is winding
a future unfolding
all speak of Your timing
moment by moment -
You know where You are going
You know where You are taking me
nothing surprises You
nothing impedes You
if I look back I falter
looking in I despair
but as I look forward
and upward
with yearning
my tiredness vanishes
my strength returns
and I understand
the need

and the speed of Your leading
and I hasten with joy
to discover the full purpose
of my pilgrimage
with You, for You,
and towards You
my Father.

(DW)

And we know that in all things God works for the good of those who love him…

Rom. 8.28

Redemption

It is your love, Lord,
that calls all creation into being

There it can be seen visible
manifest in your activity

Yet it is also in suffering
that there it lies
deeply hidden within

It is easy to see
through the beauty of nature
that you are in all things
but when I see disasters
destructive forces of nature
help me to believe
that you are there also.

I must continue to trust
and know they are part of your plan,
and to remind myself
that all things work unto good
for those who love you.

(ET)

Perfect in all your ways

Infinite
in wisdom
Almighty
in power
Perfect
in all Your ways,
In You
there is no
confusion
agitation
shifting undercurrent
change of mood
You are
the One God
- the God of order
- the eternal Ruler
- our Father
and in You alone
are found
constancy
simplicity
peace
joy
and truth.
You calm
our restless souls
You bring
Your stillness
Your certainty
Your security
into our
wild disordered lives
and in You
all things
work together
for good.

(DW)

Humble yourselves
under God's mighty hand
that he may lift
you up in due time.

1 Peter 5.6

Your hand

I think of it in a human way,
the touch of a hand,

But what when that hand
is your hand, Lord! –
always stretched out towards me
always open to give and receive,
to protect and to bless.

Help me, Lord, to hold on
to your hand which is
always there to help me.

(ET)

How ready are you?

How ready are you
to fling yourself
into my arms
your Father?
How ready are you
to trust me
not to let you fall?
How ready are you
to allow me
to clear away
all stumbling blocks
all blockages
all walls of division?
How ready are you
to allow me to
complete my task?
How ready are you
to cease all striving
to dispense
with all
unfinished business,
and every encumbrance?
When you are ready
my key will open the door
and the gates
will swing wide open
and nothing
will close them.

(DW)

Blessed is the man
that trusts in the Lord
whose confidence is in him.

He will be like a tree planted
by the water that sends
out its roots by the stream .....
it never fails to bear fruit.

Jer. 17 : 7.8

Faith

The birds created by you, Lord,
are but small,

Yet there is so much
I can learn from them

They spread their wings
with ease

And soar up high to heaven

They trust you, perfectly.

The children of this world
are placing their trust
in the things they can see,
calling them reality

Yet, Lord, you are the true reality

You bless those who trust in you
who believe without seeing

Help me to see how your heart rejoices
when I turn to you, Father
in trusting hope,

May you see my trust
as a loving gesture
to you, Lord.

(EJ)

Reality

I am surrounded by things
to see and touch and hold.
They are presented to me as reality
because they can be possessed,
assessed, reviewed, evaluated.
I may hold them, discard them,
strive for them,
bow down and worship them,
- sell my soul for them,
carry them, be burdened by them
even crushed.
These things
- these objects of desire
may hem me in,
smother me,
prop me up,
even posses me.
I may allow them
to make me feel secure.
Yet the moth and rust corrupt
and show me
that all will pass away.
The coins will slip
between my fingers.
The visible will become invisible.
The grip on all to which I cling
so firmly
will be loosened
and as comforts are withdrawn
the things I see and touch and hold
will surely fade away
and reality will confront me
the reality I have denied
and can deny no longer
- that my spirit's eye
can see more clearly
than any human sight,
that I may reach out
and touch and hold
the very hand of God

- a tangible reality
which confirms within me
a truth which will never die.
This touch, this embrace,
draws me from the poverty of my life
to the riches of His love
from the insecurity of a false and real world
to the freedom of eternity in His presence,
His real presence.

(DW)

*Blessed are the people
of whom this is true;
Blessed are the people
whose God is the Lord.*

Ps. 144 : 15

Happiness

I am only happy, Father
when I am aware of serving you.

I am only happy,
when I dwell with you
in your temple

I am only happy
when I am in union with your heart

Thank you for being the giver
of all happiness –

The kind of happiness you would
want to remain with me
until the end of my days.

(ET)

Living Lord

Great God of wonders
Creator of the
vast cosmic sweep
of all creation.
They tell me
You were then
and are not now,
That You may be there
but are not here.
But You tell me
You are with me
here, now and always.
They tell me
You are silent
but You call me
by my name.
They tell me
that You stand back
from the trivialities
and small affairs
of my daily life,
Yet You assure me
that the very hairs
on my head are numbered
and You know when
even a sparrow falls.
They tell me
there is only meaning
in the days of my existence
between my birth and death.
Yet you say to me
You knew me
in my mother's womb
and You offer me
life with You
throughout eternity.
They limit you
to non-intrusion,
non-participation,
and even non-existence.

For them You do not see,
or speak,
or touch,
or love.
Yet You are the God
who has broken
into history
and time and space
and revealed Yourself
in human form,
tangible and real,
for all to see.
You have spoken to us,
You have touched us,
You have loved us.
On the Cross of Christ
You have redeemed us
Whatever they may say.

(DW)

With the Lord a day is
like a thousand years,
and a thousand years
are like a day.

For a thousand years
in your sight
are like a day that has
just gone by.

2 Peter 3.8 & Psalm 90.4

Knowing

Give me the gift of knowing you, my Creator,
really well.

Help me to see you
not only in the pools
in the clouds and skies
in the grasses that blow in the breeze
but also in the eyes of my friends
the birds in the sky
the flowers that bloom.

In your time
a day is a thousand years
or a thousand years a day
Forever may I have the gift
of knowing you, my Creator, really well.

(ET)

Nothing

I am so small
and Your creation
vast and overwhelming.
I am so weak
and Your power
massive and infinite.
I am so sinful
and You so pure
without a single blemish.
I have no value
apart from Your imprint
on my soul.
I have no identity
apart from my name
carved on Your hand.
I have no hope
apart from Your Son
so freely given
I can do nothing
apart from Christ
nothing.

(DW)

*This is how we know we love the
children of God:
by loving God and carrying
out his commands.
This is love for God :
to obey his commands.*

1 Jn. 5 : 2-3

True Love

Lord,

You do not look for ambitious works
or expect great sacrifices from me

But you do look for love –
love that sees the need in each neighbour
love that is a friend to the loveless
love that tends the sick for no reward but love's sake
love that comforts those that need comforting
love that reaches beyond prison bars
love that spends itself in time and energy
and doesn't even recognize the cost.

Love is the greatest thing –
your word tells me so
because within love lies the power
that knows no end.

(ET)

Open my eyes

Open my eyes, Lord
to see your imprint
on each one
you lead to me,
the marks
of your fingers
on their form,
the breath
of your life
upon them,
within them.
Reveal to me
in the dignity
of their flawed
humanity
the reflection
of your beauty
and perfection.
Show me
something of you
in them
that I may
nourish it
and help it grow
and share
in some small way
your joy,
and know
you see us
not just
as we are
or appear to be
but as you always
wanted us to be.

(DW)

This is love:
not that we loved God
but that He loved us
and sent His Son as an
atoning sacrifice for our sins.

1 Jn. 4 : 10

Lord

In your love
keep me, Lord

With your trust
sustain me

With your peace
rest me

With your joy
lift me up

You are a God of love
with your love
you cover all the world

Enfold me in your love
which is warmth,
protection and light
so that I feel secure,
happy and part of you, Lord.

(ET)

A Child

Without You
I am a child deprived
of warmth and love
and Father's care
crying out
to be recognised
accepted
cherished
held
wandering
in my insecurity
seeking
and never finding
hungering
for the meal
at Your table
in Your home
in Your presence.
Invite me, Lord
welcome me
call me by my name
feed me
adopt me into Your family
enfold me in Your arms
that I may dwell
with You,
for ever
no longer orphaned
or deprived,
alone, unloved.

(DW)

Yours, O Lord, is the greatness
and the power and the glory
and the majesty and the splendour
for everything in heaven and
earth is yours.
Yours, O Lord, is the Kingdom
You are exalted as head over all.

1 Chron. 29 : 11

Glory

What is glory in the eyes
of the world?

It is something here for a moment
and then gone

It is of no lasting quality

Your glory, Lord, is eternal;
it is real
it is beautiful
it is everlasting
it reigns in heaven
and penetrates the earth
where your children belong
-   truly belong to you.

(ET)

Revelation

In the gap in the clouds
You reveal to me
Your world
as You would have it be
and the brightness
the rightness
the freshness
the goodness
the beauty
and the peace
give me hope
and joyful confidence
that the darkness
and gloom
of sick humanity
will surely pass
and all shadows
flee away.
You allow me
to see this
that I
might never allow
the deep blackness
of shame and sin
and human folly
to overwhelm me.

(DW)

Part Two

Jesus the Son:
the Name above
All names

He is the image of the invisible God, the firstborn over all creation

Col. 1.15

The Real Jesus

What is it
that
I can reach out
and touch
and, grasping,
know
that I have
taken hold
of that
which is real?
How
do I know
that
what is in
my hand
will not
wither and perish
and vanish -
ceasing to be,
becoming unreal?
Where
is the unassailable truth
which remains
when
all else has gone,
and stands secure,
which
does not depend
upon
my passing fancy,
whim
or puny intellect?
The answer
to my questions
lies not with
probes of science,
nor conjecture
of philosophy,
it is not
to be found
at all,
in human
cleverness
or destructible

matter,
but rather
in an
encounter with
the manifestation
of
absolute truth
and reality
in Jesus.
He
and no other,
stands supreme.
He
and no other
has laid down
His life
for me.
He and no other
is a sure
foundation.
Without Him
I do not know
reality.
Without Him
I will never know
the truth
which brings
freedom,
love
and life.

(DW)

Friendship

You are a precious friend, Jesus

A friend who is always at my side

A friend who is concerned
With every detail of my well-being
A friend who knows all about me
Within and without
- a friend dependable.

I regard your friendship, Jesus,
as my greatest treasure.

(ET)

God exalted him to
the highest place
and gave him the name that is
above every name,
that at the name of Jesus
every knee should bow,
in heaven and on earth and
under the earth,
and every tongue confess that
Jesus Christ is Lord,
to the glory of God the Father.

Phil. 2 : 9-11

The One who has no equal

Standing supreme
in awesome splendour
You tower over
the wrecks of time
The mighty One
subduing empires
fools and tyrants,
those who mock
and scorn Your name.
The name high over
every name
yet mocked
and ridiculed
and used
to curse.
Defiled,
abused.
Yet the power
in Your name is
beyond all powers.
You are all,
my Lord,
or absolutely nothing.
You are the victor,
or lie in crushed defeat.
Risen in Glory,
or silent and dead.
You stand supreme
or one of many.
Your words are true
or cruelly false.
You died for me
or for no one
and I know
that I cannot
turn away
or hide from You
in words, in concepts
or in crowds.
I cannot for ever
fool myself
or others
about the nature
of Your reality,

Your Lordship.
I must deny - take up the hammer and the nails
or in full obedience
and subjection
kneel
before the One
who has no equal.

(DW)

Power

Your's Lord is the power
and the glory.

Mine is the freedom of choice;

I carry your Name on my lips,
the Name of Jesus.

Consequently all evil
is rendered powerless

Thank you, Lord.

(ET)

You have made known to
me the path of life,
You will fill me with joy
in your presence,
with eternal pleasures
at your right hand.

Ps. 16 : 11

A Walk to Heaven

You come to us
You call to us
to gather us together
to be close to You
and one another.
You call us by name
to be with You
and each other
to be Your Body in the world
Your real and living presence.
You call us to be instruments
of healing and serving
of loving and forgiving.
Your way is the way
of the simple and the poor
Your words are words of hope
to a hopeless world.
They are words of life
to a life-denying world
You speak the liberating truth
which sets us free
to walk with You to Heaven.

(DW)

Everything

You, Lord, are the bright morning star,
the Alpha and Omega

You are all that is good
and perfect
and everlasting

Glory, splendour, majesty
are but weak words
when describing your attributes

May nothing distract me
from centering my life on you,
from living the more excellent way
following you always.

(ET)

God is light. In him there is
no darkness at all....

1 Jn. 1 : 5

In him was life,
and that life was the light of men.
The light shines in the darkness
but the darkness has not understood it.

Jn. 1 : 4-5

Resurrection Truth

You call us
to reveal You
to a disbelieving world.
You call us
to be Your presence
in the emptiness of life.
You call us
to be Your body
seen, touched and recognised.
You call us
to show
the reality of
Your presence
that the world might see
and proclaim
with all creation
You are risen
You are risen indeed.

(DW)

Pure Light

I bring to you my dark places, Lord,
for you to shine your light into them –
into all areas of need.

You are the light of the world,

Your light can change the look of creation,
can in fact change the function of nature.

May I be touched by your light
that shines in the darkness,

May I be enfolded in that same light
that cannot be extinguished

The light – your light – you now shine into me
illumines my mind,
raises my spirit
and gives wings to my soul;

Your light is sometimes likened to the sun,
and no wonder!

Because the sun is powerful and bright,
warm and purifying,
penetrating and life giving

However, one thing differs;
Your light is everlasting.

(ET)

You did not choose me,
but I chose you and
appointed you to go and
bear fruit - fruit that will last.

Jn. 15 : 16

You Chose Me

You trace my coming
through all
the tortuous channels
of the generations.
Each tributary
and stream.
You know
each confluence
making me
what I now am.
The flickering torch
passed on through
hidden family years
burst forth
into a blaze that day
when You ordained
that I should live.
The tree
with deep, deep roots
nurtured by Your Spirit
in all the ages
knew many
joyous summers
and many
long bleak winters.
It knew the
gentle sadness
of the Fall.
Yet in fresh Spring
its branches
reaching ever out
and up
produced the bud
that You decreed
would be my life.
It was no random chance
You chose,
You gave,
and ever since
Your hand
has been
upon my life
that it may be
a season of fruitfulness

that it may reflect
Your glory,
that in its nothingness
and all its imperfection
it may become
one day
something beautiful
for You
and may this
for ever be
my joy
my comfort:
I did not choose You
You chose me.

(DW)

You Ask

You ask, Lord,
for me to provide the fertile soil
for you to sow your seeds.

You ask that I water –
and feed them
with my prayers

Then you will see
that they blossom
and bear fruit.

(ET)

*Speaking the truth in love, we will in
all things grow up into him who is the
Head, that is Christ. From him the
whole body joined and held together
by every supporting ligament, grows
and builds itself up in love,
as each part does its work.*

Eph. 4 : 15-16

His Living Body

You call us
to join
one with another
as members
of Your living Body
moving in unison
revealing
to the world
the harmony
of Your love,
the reality
of Your presence,
Your Spirit
breathed upon us,
Your life
and healing
flowing through us,
so that
when men, women
and children
see us
they see
You
Jesus
alive
here now.

(DW)

Heart of Fire

The Body of Christ today – your Body, Jesus-
is your loving Heart in the world

A heart that beats with compassion
for all creatures and all creation

A heart in which you offer a place
to everyone who wishes to join you,

A heart that is the centre point
of all activity and energy
of any kind of good,

A heart which is like a fire
a fire that burns away the chaff,
a fire that in its love
holds all the children of the world
a fire that warms the coldest heart
and never goes out

Lord, may I hold within me
the spark that sets alight
a fire in my heart,
a holy fire that burns up chaff
that refines and purges
until there is nothing but purity
and all to Your Heart's delight.

(ET)

I am the true vine, and my Father is the gardener. He cuts off every branch in me that bears no fruit, while every branch that does bear fruit he prunes so that it will be even more fruitful....I am the vine you are the branches.

Jn. 15 : 1-2

Who are we?

We are Your people, Lord
called and gathered in Your name
bonded by Your love
walking together,
travelling light.
We are Your flock, Lord
the sheep of Your pasture
to whom the shepherd's voice is known.
We are Your family, Lord
beloved children
delighting in the unity
and warmth of oneness
in Your Fatherhood.
We are the branches
You are the life-giving vine
sustaining, feeding,
enabling us to bear Your fruit.
We are Your body, Christ,
knitted, joined together
to be Your presence
fulfil Your healing work
tell of Your Kingdom.
Yet we are the hungry
and You are the Bread of Life.
We are the thirsty
and You are Living Water.
We have dwelt in darkness
and You are the Light of the World.
We are the lost
and You have found us.
We are weary
and You give us rest.
We are the crucifiers
and You cry 'Father forgive!'
Help us to know in fullness
our true identity
made in Your image
filled with Your Spirit
born to be free
called to serve
loved with an everlasting love.

(DW)

Come to me, all you who are weary and burdened, and I will give you rest. Take my yoke upon you and learn from me, for I am gentle and humble in heart, and you will find rest for your souls. For my yoke is easy and my burden is light.

Mt. 11 : 28-30

I Come to Jesus

I come to the One
who has the name
above all names
I bow before Him
for never have I known
such purity
such perfect love
such manifest truth
Here is the One
who towers over all,
in might and majesty
in awesome tenderness
and peace
beyond all words
beyond compare
alone
unique
Jesus.

(DW)

The Quest

Help me, Lord
not to be restless
unless I am restless for your word
not to be impatient
unless I am impatient for meeting with you
not to be dissatisfied unless I am dissatisfied
in not finding what my heart is searching for.

Your word tells me to seek
and I shall find —
this is your promise.

(ET)

…be my rock of refuge,
a strong fortress to save me.
Since you are my rock
and my fortress,
for the sake of your name
lead and guide me.

Ps.31 : 2b-3

…they drank from the
spiritual rock that
accompanied them,
and that rock was Christ.

1 Cor. 10 : 4

Trust

If I do not
place my trust
in God
on whom
do I rely?
If He is not
the rock
on which
I build
what are my
real foundations?
If He is not
the fixed centre
of my life
what is?
Surely if I rely
on me
or others
I am deluded.
Surely if I am founded
on any other
than the Lord
I am
on sinking sand.
Surely if He
is not at the heart
of my life
there is a void,
a nothingness
an emptiness
and I am lost.

(DW)

Assurance

Jesus, you are my Rock

However strong the winds
of fortune may try to blow
me off course,
clinging to you, the Rock,
my rescue is assured.

In the safety of the rock
I am invincible;
though on my own
I would be as frail as grass,
clinging to you, the Rock, will make
me rock-like.

(ET)

Those who hope in the Lord
will renew their strength.
They will soar on wings
like eagles....

Is. 40 : 31

The Truth which sets me free

Your touch is pure,
as bright as crystal,
sharp and clear
without blemish
or fault,
untarnished,
shining
for ever unsubdued
contrasting
to the drab
and deadly dimness
of a benighted, ugly world
of lies
and darkness
from which
you wish
to set me free.

(DW)

Eagle

I would be content,
to remain like Your little dove, Lord
serving you quietly and devotedly

But I sense you would have me
spread my wings
and transform your little dove
into a mighty eagle.

An eagle has much to teach me:
He does not question
or wonder
or philosophise
He just flies and does what comes naturally.

You created him king of the birds
with a capacity for flight
that surpasses all others
His flight is majestic,
His movements graceful

He glides on the air
and dives for his prey
with tremendous speed and accuracy
His nest is built high though hidden
and his strength is greater
than that of other birds
when gliding on thermals

We can remain effortless in flight
relaxing, resting, surrendered
with a single-minded concentration

Whatever action is required
comes after stillness –
the resting again,
circling on thermals
before further action.

Lord Jesus, grant me
the will and generosity
to allow you to transform me
into the eagle of your choice.

(EI)

Let us fix our eyes on Jesus,
the author and perfector of our faith,
who for the joy set before him
endured the cross, scorning its shame,
and sat down at the right hand
of the throne of God.

Heb. 12 : 2

Standing Alone

You call me to stand alone
without the shield of approbation,
lacking the safe protection of the crowd,
alone to feel the wind upon my face,
alone to be vulnerable, easily hurt.
And in my solitary walk
You take me to the place
where I can see with new perspective
the far-off scene
of which I was and am a part.
And in my silence
I hear the murmuring of the crowd
the ceaseless round of human striving
which would absorb, coerce,
control, consume me.
And in my loneliness -
I feel the danger and dismay.
I pay the price of nonconformity
willingly, but not without some fear.
Then suddenly I am aware
of Your presence, silent, still and strong.
My despised, reviled and hated Master
In prayer. At peace.
Seeing all. Loving all
even those who reject you
Understanding all, forgiving all
even those who would crucify You.
And as you let me see You
and stand with You
in my utter unworthiness
I am no longer alone.

(DW)

Triumph

I look upon your cross, Jesus
and what do I see?
only love
only life
only hope and deep compassion.

No more death

No more sin

No more fear.

(ET)

Is not the cup of thanksgiving
for which we give thanks
a participation in the
blood of Christ?
And is not the bread that
we break a participation in
the Body of Christ?

1 Cor. 10 : 16

Bread

While the masses
in their spiritual hunger
cry for food,
the granaries of God
are full to overflowing
and we His people
who ourselves are hungry
hold the locks
and keys
which could unleash
the sustenance
and nourishment
to save
and feed
a starving, dying world
of which we are a part.

Jesus says, -
"I am the bread of life".

(DW)

Revelation

Whosoever has difficulty in finding you, Lord,
they will always find you at the altar-rail

No-one can substitute for you

When we come to share your Broken Body
amongst us, we can never be surer
of your Presence with us.

Help us to believe this
and to keep this knowledge
in our heart and mind
and to be aware of this big thing
you do for us and in us
as we come in faith and reach out to you.

Lord, you long
to open our eyes
to this wonderful thing you do for us all
so very, very much.

(ET)

Be self-controlled and alert.
Your enemy the devil prowls around
like a roaring lion looking
for someone to devour.
Resist him standing firm
in the faith.

1 Pe. 5 : 8-9

Conflict

You send me to the battlefield
when I would sooner stay at home
You place me in the firing line
when I yearn to be at peace
You put me into conflict
when I am weary of all wars
You show me all the ugliness -
corruption, lies, deceit
of crooked men who triumph
when the weak are trampled down.
You point me to injustice
to poverty and greed
and powers of darkness gathering
to pollute, ensnare, destroy.
How can I be impassive
when the struggle is so severe?
And the powers arraigned against the Lord
cause so much pain and fear?
But the battle and the victory are
Yours and Yours alone
and all demons fear and fly
at the mention of your name.
For you who are so close to us
are greater by far
than the one who is against
and truth and love will triumph
by the might of Your great power.

(DW)

Victory

Lord Jesus,
It is you who confronts and rebukes the evil one

None but you deals with the evil spirits completely

They know your voice and fear you
They struggle but it is to no avail
It is your love for us that has won the victory
and thus overcomes all evil forces.
Still they continue to torment
the unsuspecting, unprotected, unprepared;
but we, your children, are prepared
for any battle.

We are equipped with the battle gear
and our protection is that we believe in you

Your Name is upon our hearts
and when it flows from our lips
it is like a battle cry
which no demon can withstand
but must flee and be banished forever.

Thank you, Lord Jesus,
that we are your soldiers,
your instruments, your channels
from whom and through which
you command your law
which is a law of love.

(ET)

If anyone loves me, he will obey my teaching. My Father will love him and we will come to him and make our home with him.

Jn. 14 : 23

Coming

You come to me
gently
imperceptibly
beautifully
as the early morning sun
stealing
silently upon me.
The freshness of Your light -
its tender brightness
quietly unfolding,
revealing again
the ever-changing
silent beauty of
what you have made
and are making,
brings me
Your deep peace
confirmed by
the long shadows,
the freshness of the dew
the chatter of
the early rising birds
the gentle misty colours
and your loving breath
upon my soul -
this speaks to me
in wordless wonder of
Your patient, forbearing,
caring, persistent
and ever present
love.

(DW)

Humble King

You who are mightiest

The King of all Kings

do not come with great pomp

You come to me in the gentle breeze

like a shadow

falling over me

quietly

in the stillness of my heart.

If I expect you, Jesus,

You will be there.

(ET)

Part Three

The Holy Spirit:
Our life-giver

…Whoever drinks the water I give him will never thirst again. Indeed, the water I give him will become in him a spring of water welling up to eternal life.

Jn. 4 : 14

The Spring

Your Spirit, the spring
of power and goodness
will never stop flowing

It is available to all
who cry out in need.

I cry out to you now, Lord,
in my need.

Immerse me in your Spirit,
Totally cover me

Bathe me in it
purify me
as I surface make me
newly open
newly teachable
newly touchable.

(ET)

Why?

The rising sap
The bursting bud
The fresh green shoot
The bird on the wing
Gurgling mountain streams
The urgent chatter
of little children
and the ripple of laughter,
all these tell me
of the gift of life
in all its abundance
which the Lord pours forth
upon all creatures
and all creation
with joy.
Why, then
with all this colour
and the prospect
of vibrant living
overflowing
with the excitement
of newness,
why do we choose the death
of a godless life
spurning the giver,
choosing darkness
in place of life?

(DW)

May the God of hope
fill you with all joy and peace
as you trust in him, so that you may
overflow with hope by the
power of the Holy spirit.

Rom. 15 : 13

The Temple of the Holy Spirit

You do not invade
the privacy
of the house
which is my life.
You do not intrude
into the rooms
which are the domain
of my soul.
You do not impose
Your presence
upon the hidden
and unwelcoming
spaces of my being
You stand,
patiently
lovingly
sadly
waiting
for my response
to your knocking
waiting
for my invitation
for You to enter
into my life
as a welcome guest
to open
my whole being
to Your presence
that I may become
Your abiding place,
the Temple
of the Holy Spirit

(DW)

86

Reign in me

Lord God,

As you dwell in three persons
in the Holy Trinity

So also you dwell threefold
in heaven on high
in the souls of your loved ones
and in the world all around us.

Your power and goodness
are everywhere,
there is nothing or no-one
that can destroy you

How grateful I am
that your love and goodness
reign forever

You reign in your heavenly Kingdom, Lord

You reign on earth below

But what you covet most of all
is to reign in the hearts of your people

Enthrone me in your heart and then
I shall be pleasing unto your eye.

(ET)

Step by Step

Step by step
as I approach You
the silence
becomes deeper,
the light
becomes brighter.
I shed my words
discard my loads
set aside
all concepts
ideas, questions
and tribulation.
I approach a Purity
in which there is
no imperfection.
I approach a Presence
which overwhelms,
timeless,
awesome,
complete
all-loving
all-powerful
almighty
and my eyes
are opened,
my ears
unstopped
and I am lost
in wonder
in love
and praise.

(DW)

If the Son sets you free
You will be free indeed

Jn. 8 : 36

Be Free

The clouds are free
to roam the sky

The waves of the ocean
flow where they will

The rivers rush
where they are led.

You would have me free
to move in your Spirit
and for your love to hold me, Lord.

Grant me a free spirit,
a spirit that is not bound
to routine
a spirit that is flexible
to bend with your purposes,
a spirit that is not tied
to my own will
but to Yours.

(ET)

A Mighty Blast of Trumpets

There is a stillness
and heavy foreboding,
the air is filled
with sombre expectation.
The enemy is prowling
like a wild and vicious animal
ever ready to pounce.
The armies of darkness
remorselessly approach.
Their advanced cohorts
have entered the city gates
Their collaborators are busy
destroying the city walls
and the Temple
lies in the ruins of neglect,
despair, decay and desolation.
The waiting will soon be over.
The ominous silence
will soon be rudely broken.
Soon the mighty assault
will be mounted.
The drum beats,
marching feet
and shrieks of battle
will be heard.
But now,
in this prolonged pause
as some woken sleepers
tremble fearfully
a mighty blast of trumpets
will be heard -
warning the city
breaking its unnatural peace,
disturbing those cocooned
in comfort and complacency,
sounding the alarm,
rallying the people,
marshalling the warriors of God,
equipping the saints for battle,
announcing the Coming of the Lord
who is mighty and victorious
and against whom

no one and no thing
can prevail.
Lord, prepare me
clothe me,
arm me
protect me
from all subterfuge
and evil ways,
and give me
a quiet heart
that can face the future
with no fear
but a simple trust
that He who is with us
will remain with us
and is stronger, by far,
than the one
who is against us,
who in spite of
his arrogance,
his ruthlessness,
his cunning
and his wealth
will be flung down
from his place of power,
no more
to trample on the weak
no more
to bring sadness and grief.
The One who is with us
is mighty in war
but we welcome Him
even now, not just as victor, but
as Prince of Peace.

(DW)

*With joy you will
draw water from
the wells of salvation.*

Is. 12 : 3

Deep Well

Your love, Lord, is like a deep deep well
that will never run dry

I can take as much water as I like
but will never reach the bottom
and it will never seem less.

May I be like that Lord

May I be a being of great depth

May I be able to reach greater depths
in that well within me.

Then I shall be able to give more water
and more of your joy
to those I meet.

Joy is like bubbling water
it has strength
it has force
it has power

It will not be contained.

Lord, may Your joy – the joy of Your Holy Spirit -
flow from me

May it spread all around so as to affect everyone I meet.

(ET)

His nearness

Alone
in silence
waiting
for sounds
of Your coming,
listening
in deep depths
of stillness
I find
myself
at this
noiseless
timeless
point
beyond
all striving
and all thought,
subdued
and filled
with awe,
feeling
the breath
of Yahweh
on my life,
knowing
His presence
in the
quietness
of my soul.

(DW)

Now to him who is able to do immeasurably more than we can ask or imagine, according to his power that is at work within us, to him be glory in the Church and in Christ Jesus throughout all generations, for ever and ever. Amen.

Eph. 3 : 20-21

Living Power

Fire and water
are two mighty elements
with which you, Lord,
compare your Holy Spirit.

Yet your Holy Spirit
is far mightier than that.

Help me to become aware
of the immense power
that lies within me –
the immense power
that I have access to –
the power that is part
of the Holy Trinity
and is forever.

(ET)

Veni Sancte Spiritus

Holy Spirit
I tremble
in asking
for Your coming
for I know
that You will
lead me
along paths
I do not wish to take -
into the desert,
through the darkness,
knowing despair,
rejection,
loneliness,
hunger,
fear,
burdened with
temptation
guilt
and unbelief,
attacked
on all sides,
wounded,
stumbling
to the very point
of losing myself
and everything
I hold dear
only to find
the fiery presence
of my
Living Lord,
who comes
at the
penultimate moment
to warm
my coldness
and breathe
His very being
into my heart.

(DW)

O God, you are my God,
earnestly I seek you;
My soul thirsts for you,
in a dry and weary land
where there is no water.

Ps. 63 : 1

Thirsting

Lord, I see myself
as a dry, barren valley,
cracked and dying

There is an obstruction
to the entrance of the valley
and it is THIRST that removes it –
a dying thirst for you, Lord.

The thirst breaks down the obstruction
and your waters rush in
and flood the valley
and transform the dry, cracked earth
into rich yielding soil
where the seeds may grow in abundance

The valley overflows with a richness of life.

May I thirst and thirst again
for you, my Lord and life-giver.

(ET)

Our Cry

We cry out
for healing
of our diseases
Yet we go,
seeking refreshment
from poisoned fountains
and drink deeply
of contamination.
We cry out
for guidance
and help
from those
who are themselves
lost, troubled
and confused.
We cry out
for the truth
yet consult
false prophets
with their easy
half-truths and
comfortable lies.
But if we cried
to the Lord
the healer
of all diseases,
the provider
of pure living water
the one who is
the way, the truth
the life -
we would not cry
in vain.

(DW)

I pray…that all of them may be one,
Father, just as you are
in me and I am in you…
I have given them the glory
that you gave me, that they
may be one as we are one…
May they be brought
to complete unity
to let the world know
that you sent me…

Jn. 17 : 21-23

Unity

Jesus, you prayed to your Father
that all should be one
so that the world would believe
that you are the One the Father sent.

It is urgent and important –
all need to be one
or the world cannot believe

There are many parts
but only one Body.

When parts come together in harmony
there is found fullness of joy.

The strength of a united body
is like that of a strong oak tree
which does not yield to the temptations
of the elements.

O Jesus, if all your children
would be one,
then much of your aching heart
would be healed

Hasten that day, O Holy Spirit

At Pentecost you united all the nations
of the world
made them hear and understand

In the same way,
may you, O Holy Spirit,
be with us today
breaking down any divisions,
uniting your Church.

May you dwell in all the hearts
of your people
so that they shall all be one.
(ET)

Oneness

When you are truly
One with Me
You will not rest until
You are one
with all my people
everywhere.
Until
all walls of division
come tumbling down
and every barricade
is cast aside
and My flock
is gathered in,
and the chicks
are no longer scattered,
and My family
meeting in joy
in love
in unity
around the one table
sharing the one loaf.
This, My children
will bring joy
to My heart
and then
the world
will begin
to believe.

(DW)

*I have come that they
may have life and
have it to the full.*

Jn. 10 : 10

Eternally New

Lord,
Your life is new life
-   new life every moment that you come to me.

'Tis the same life that goes on forever
and yet it is new.

As the night covers all the hurts of the day,
so your presence comes to me as peace
and gives me new beginning.

(ET)

Lord of all Life

Lord of all Life,
Be my Lord,
Be my Life.
To live is to grow,
To know
In greater measure
- your love
- your peace
- your joy.
Help me to grow
- to blossom
- to bear fruit.
In growing take from me
- the lazy, stubborn heart
- the fear of change
- the dread of the unknown.
In growing
- set my pace
- be it fast or slow.
May I be for ever knowing your life, your love
- in greater measure
- in richer treasure.

(DW)

After the earthquake came a fire, but the Lord was not in the fire. And after the fire came a gentle whisper ....

1 Kings 19 : 12

The Still Small Voice

The lies of the world
are shouted loud
and repeated noisily
remorselessly
emphatically
dogmatically
and we allow them
to echo
and to resonate
within our minds
and hearts
until we hardly hear
the still small voice
speaking quietly,
persistently,
lovingly,
speaking the truth
which remains,
and is eternal.
This truth
which in its purity
and simplicity
shines brightly
in a dark,
confused and wicked world
choking to death
on its own lies,
ensnared in its web of deceit.
This voice,
though, still and small,
can never be denied
or silenced.
It is the voice of God.

(DW)

A Prayer

Lord I pray
that I may allow You
to fill me,
to feed and refresh me,
and that I may experience
Your love and tenderness
in a new and deeper way.
I pray that I may discover
my value in Your sight
and in loving You
know in greater measure
Your will and Your ways.
I ask that at all times
I may be able
to keep my hands open
to receive what
You so much want to give
to me
and to know your joy
and encouragement
wherever I am
whatever I am doing
whatever my thoughts
whatever my feelings.

(DW)

Jesus said: "I praise you, Father, Lord of heaven and earth, because you have hidden these things from the wise and learned, and revealed them to little children. Yes, Father, for this was your good pleasure.

Mt. 11 : 25

Who am I?

The question is daunting and haunting.
As day follows day
And year follows year.
As feeling, encounters
and movements and meetings
and dreams and visions
and desires and decisions
come, and as quickly, go,
Transient and fragile
Who am I?
Surely more than one
bearing just the imprints and bruises,
the marks of a cruel, contriving world?
Am I not more than the fruit
of my Age?
Or the fruit of the ages
of families long passed?
In my solitude I ask myself
Who am I?
This moment
At this place
I am not the one
those around me see
I am not the person
I believe myself to be
I am not the person I was
nor the one I'm, going to be.
So who am I?
Bearing this image
Wearing these masks
Playing this role
So busy living
Coming and going
Watching and listening
Seeking - not finding?
Recalling, regretting
beset with all manner of faults
and impurities
Failing and falling
Fumbling and fearing
Yet I am the one
into whom you have breathed your life
and to whom you have given your spirit.

No chance molecular encounter
But designed and ordained
to be in your image
reflecting your presence
living your being.
This is who I am.
The one you name and love
Now in all eternity.

(DW)

The Maranatha Community is a movement of thousands of
Christians drawn from all the churches in the United Kingdom
and is committed to praying and working for Christian Unity,
Christian Healing and Christian Renewal.
It is committed to prayer and action.

*"Be prepared to be stopped, searched and supported as you travel the pilgrim way
with this encouraging resource of prayer poems."*
The Revd. Dr. Russ Parker, Director of Acorn Christian Foundation,

*"This book has come not from the pen of those who simply talk about Prayer,
but vessels who have experienced God in and through prayer.
My prayer is that each reader will experience the power of the risen
Christ as you meditatively read this book."*
Wale Babatunde, Senior Minister, World Harvest Christian Centre; Founder
Christian Heritage & Reformation Trust (CHRT)

*'If you pray without serving, your prayer will be in vain.
If you serve without praying, your service will be in vain.
Go forward - pray and serve in the power of the Holy Spirit'.*
- a message from Mother Teresa of Calcutta to the Maranatha Community

The Maranatha Community
102 Irlam Road, Flixton, Manchester M41 6JT
Tel: 0161 748 4858 Fax 0161 747 7379
Email: info@maranathacommunity.org.uk
www.maranathacommunity.org.uk